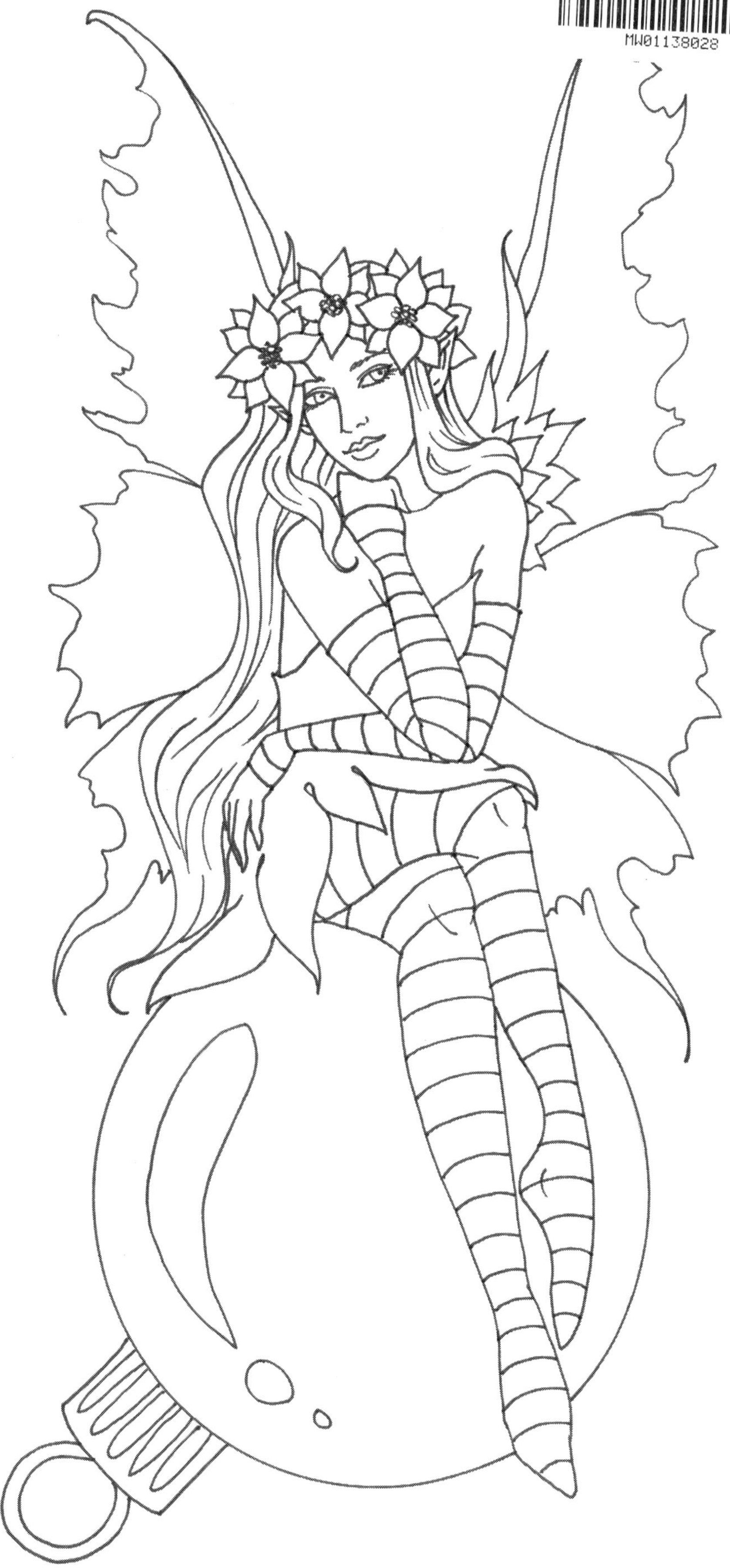

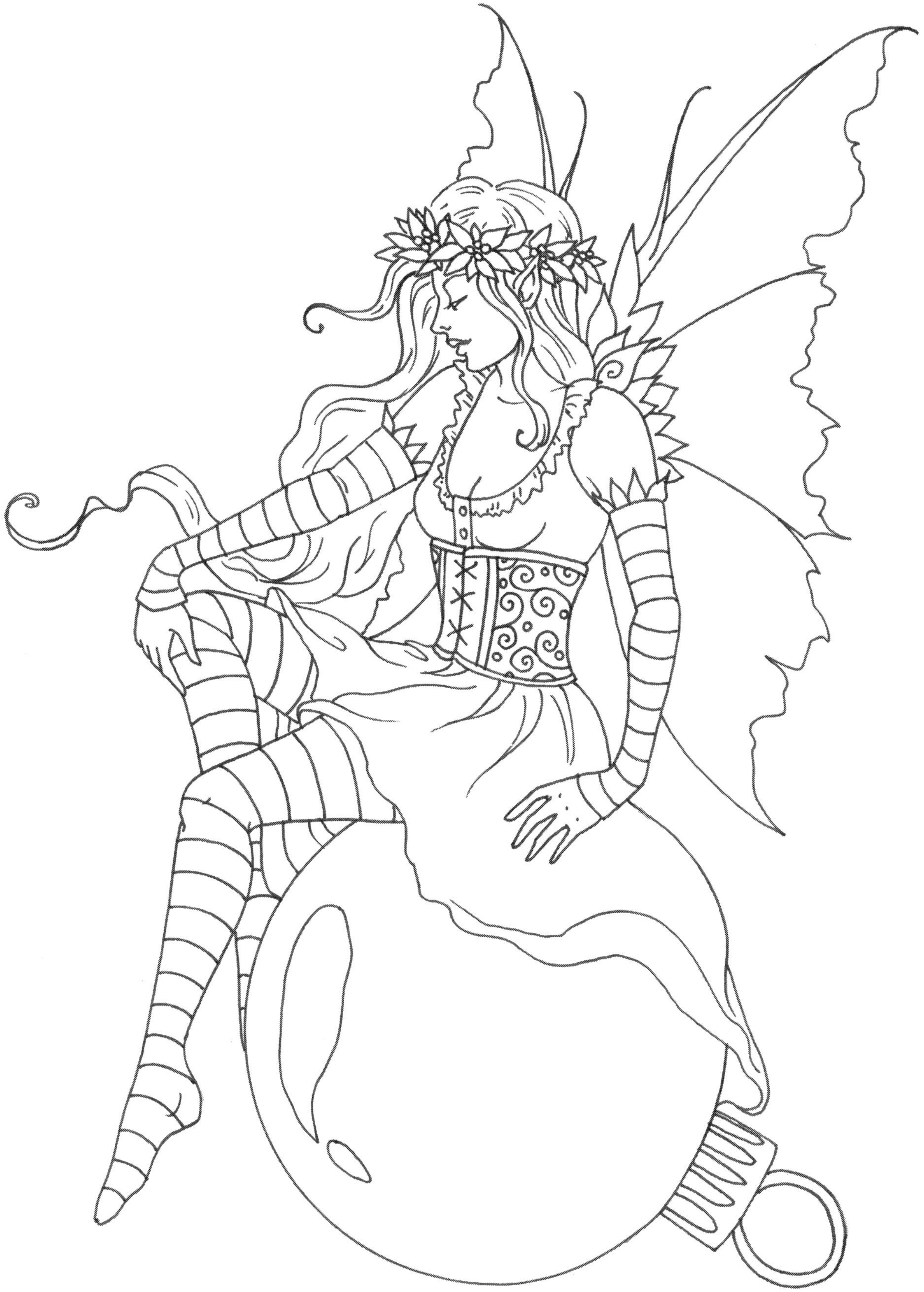

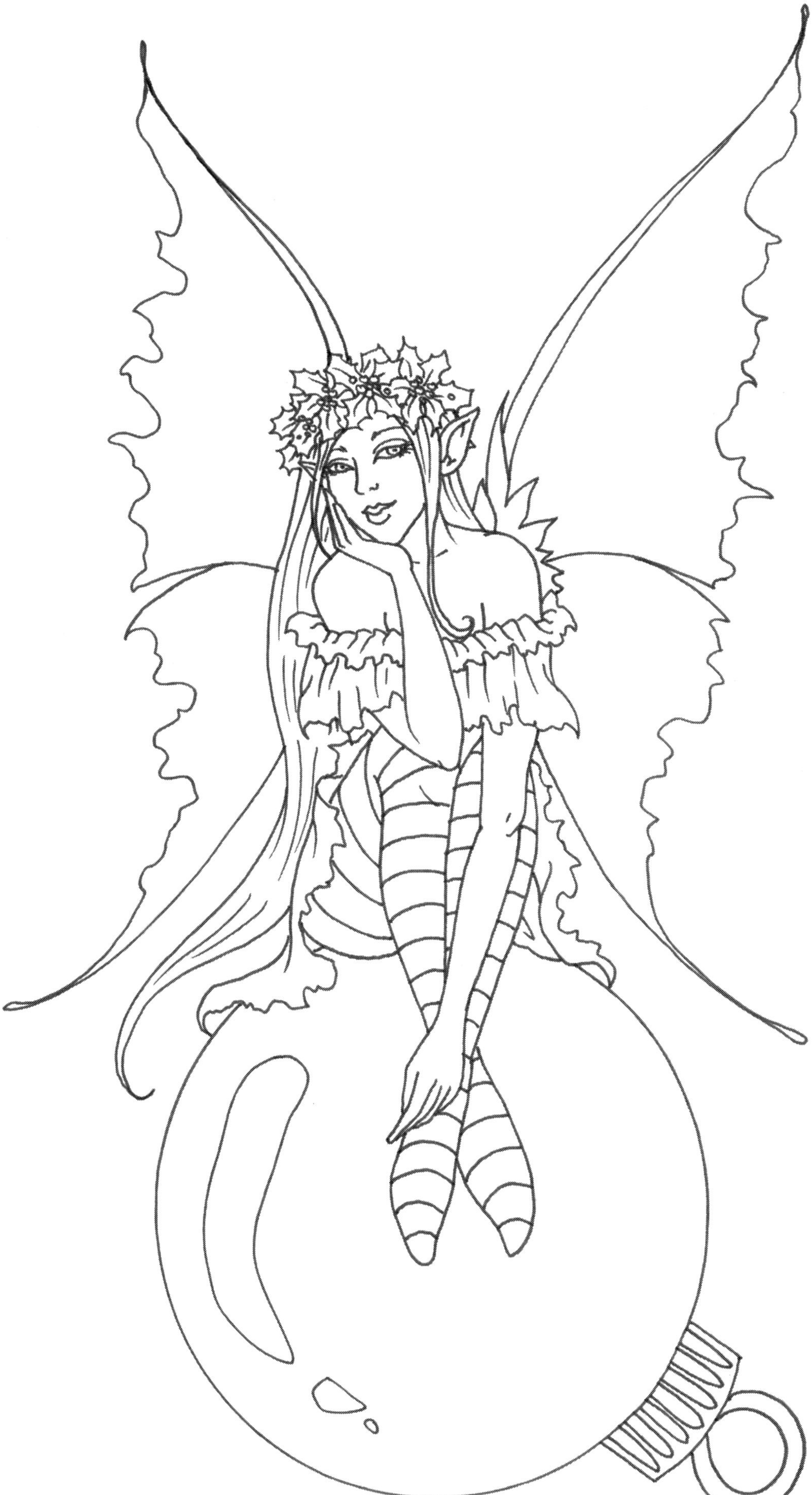

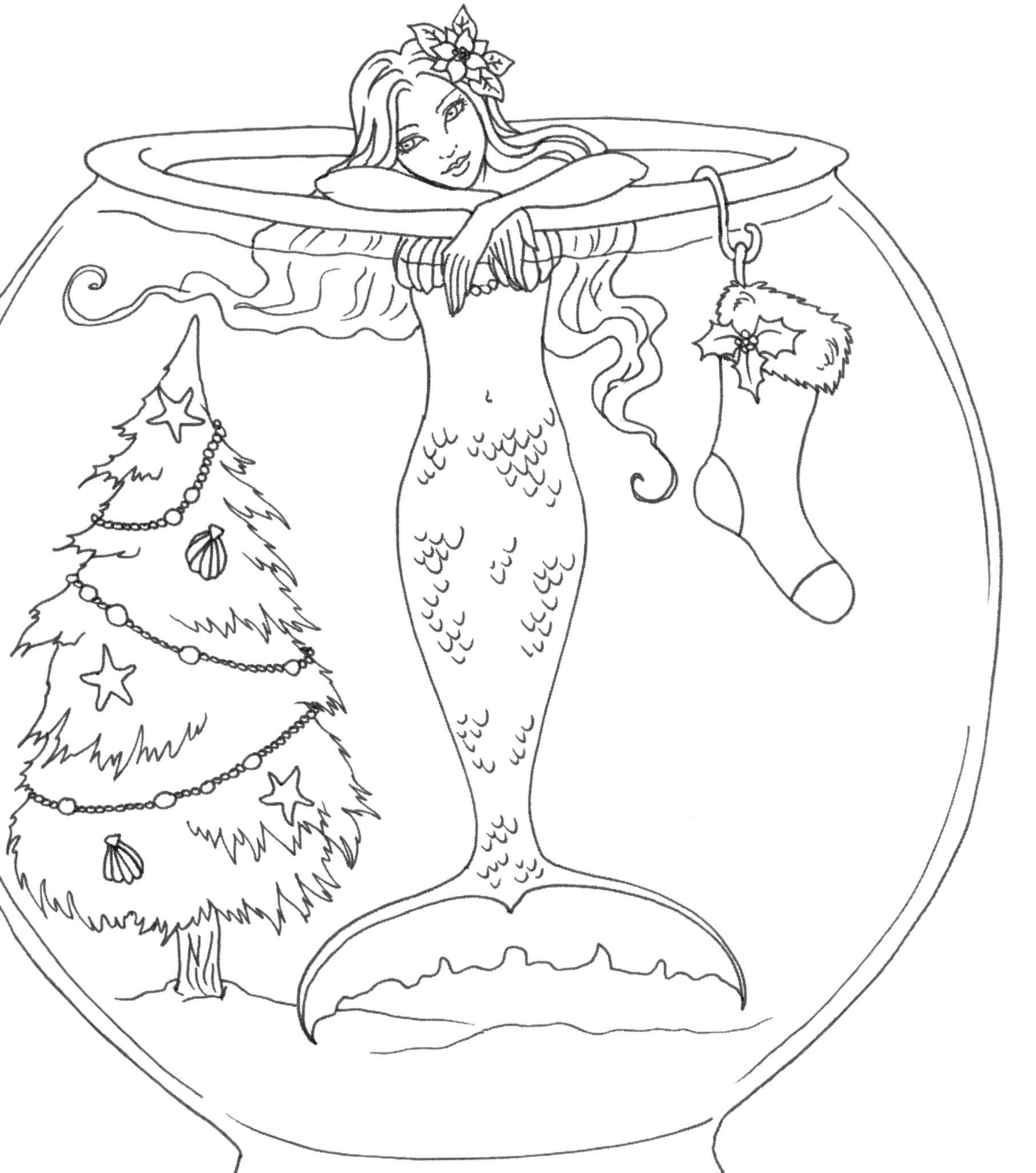

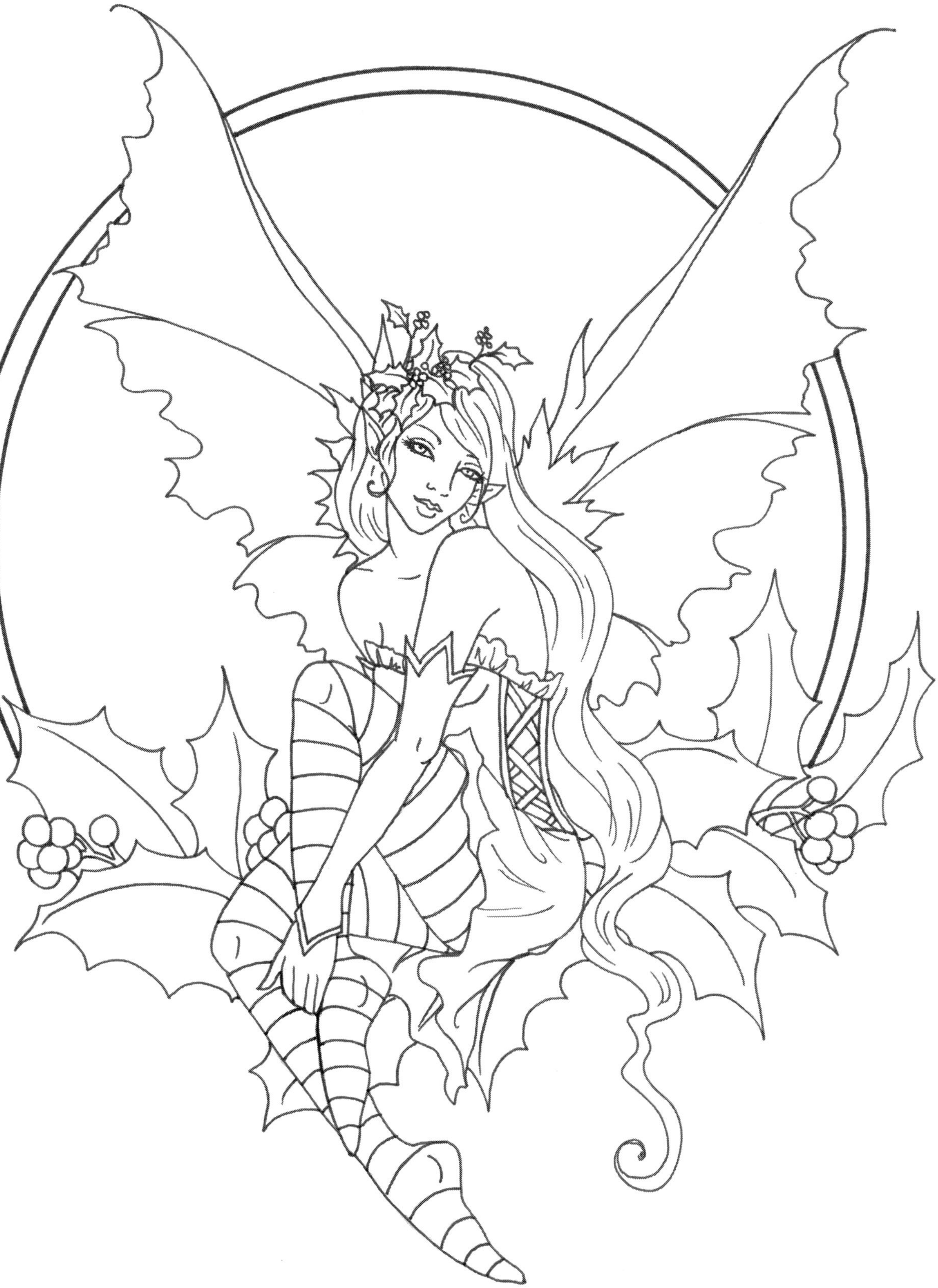

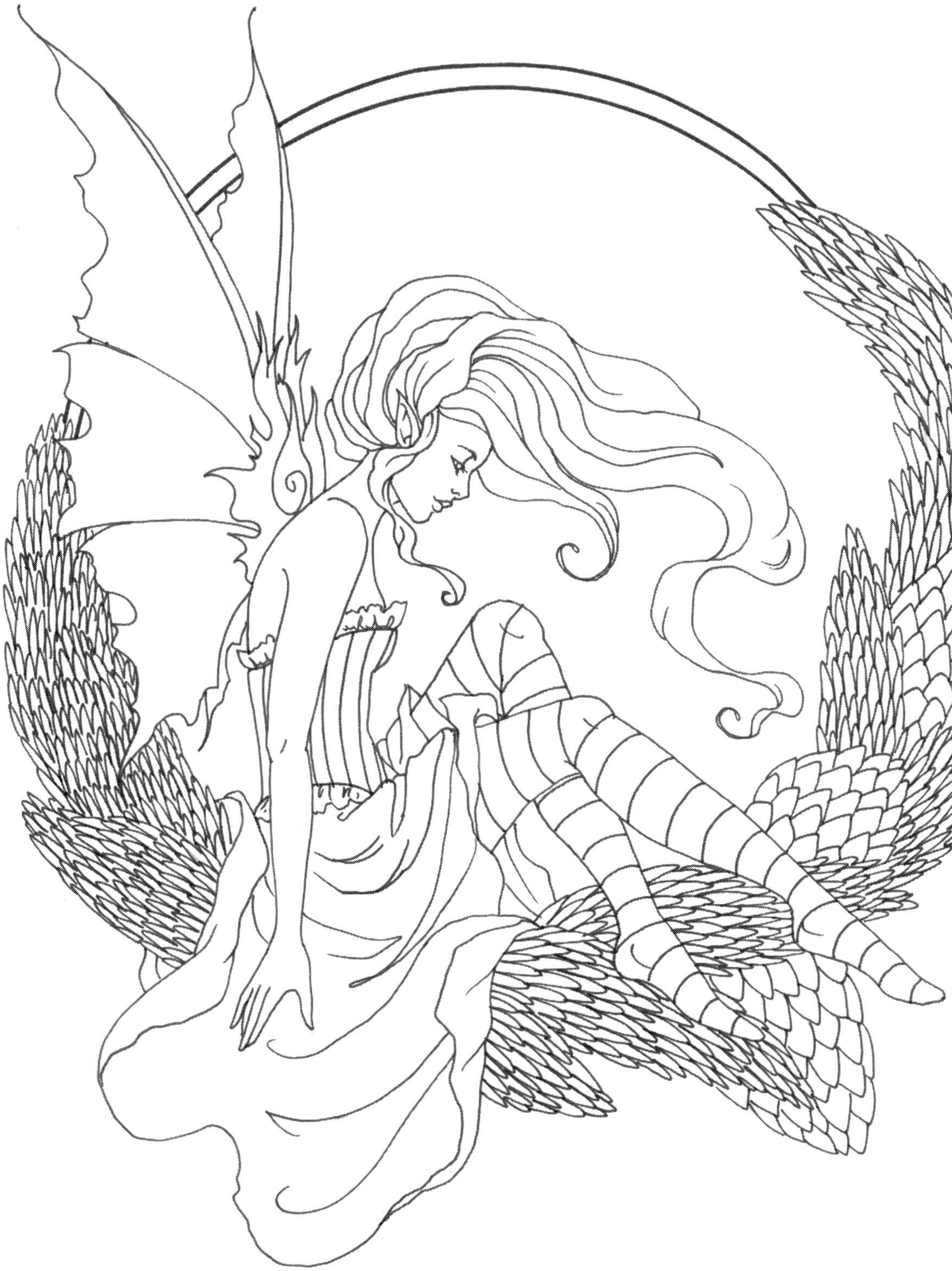

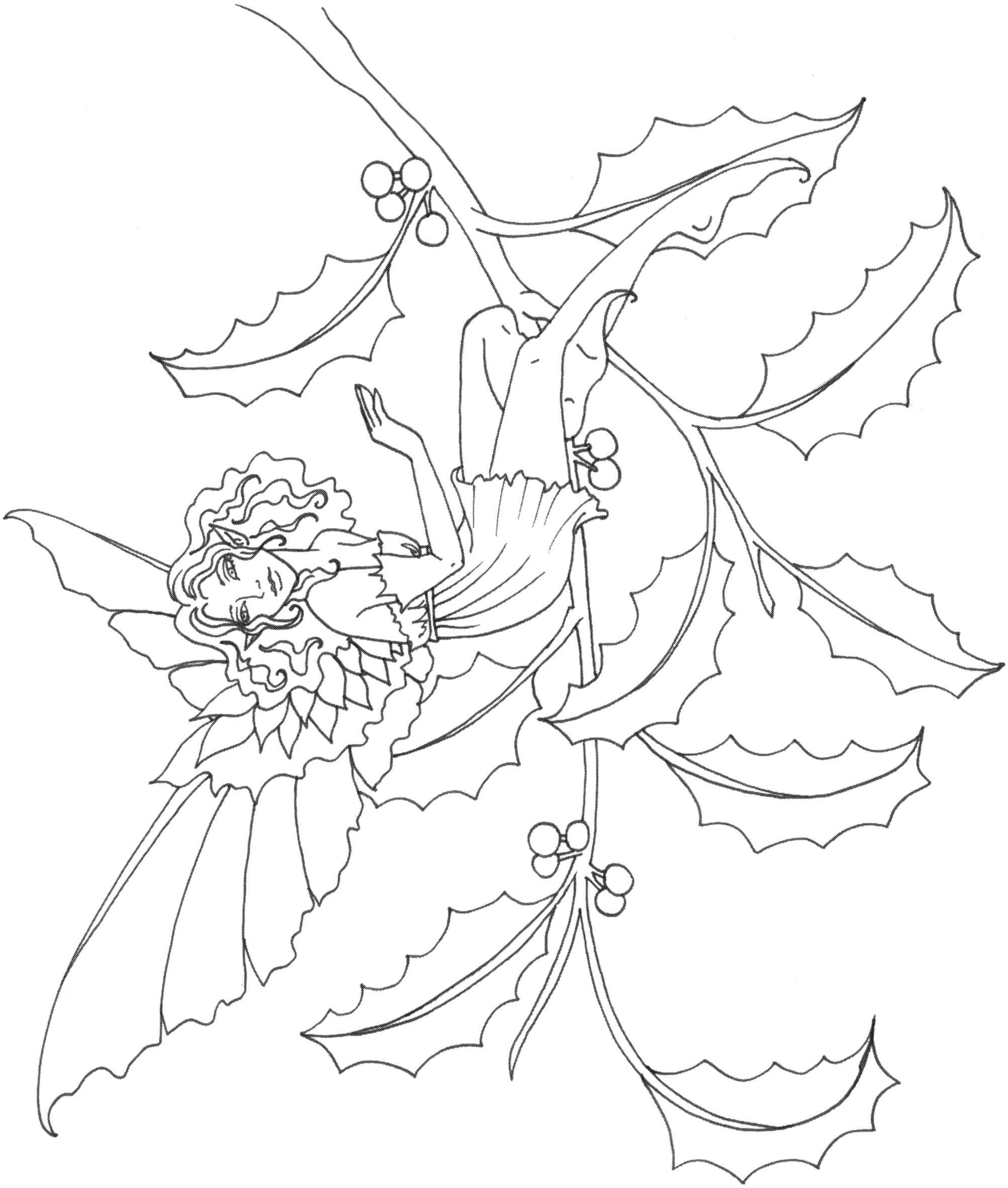

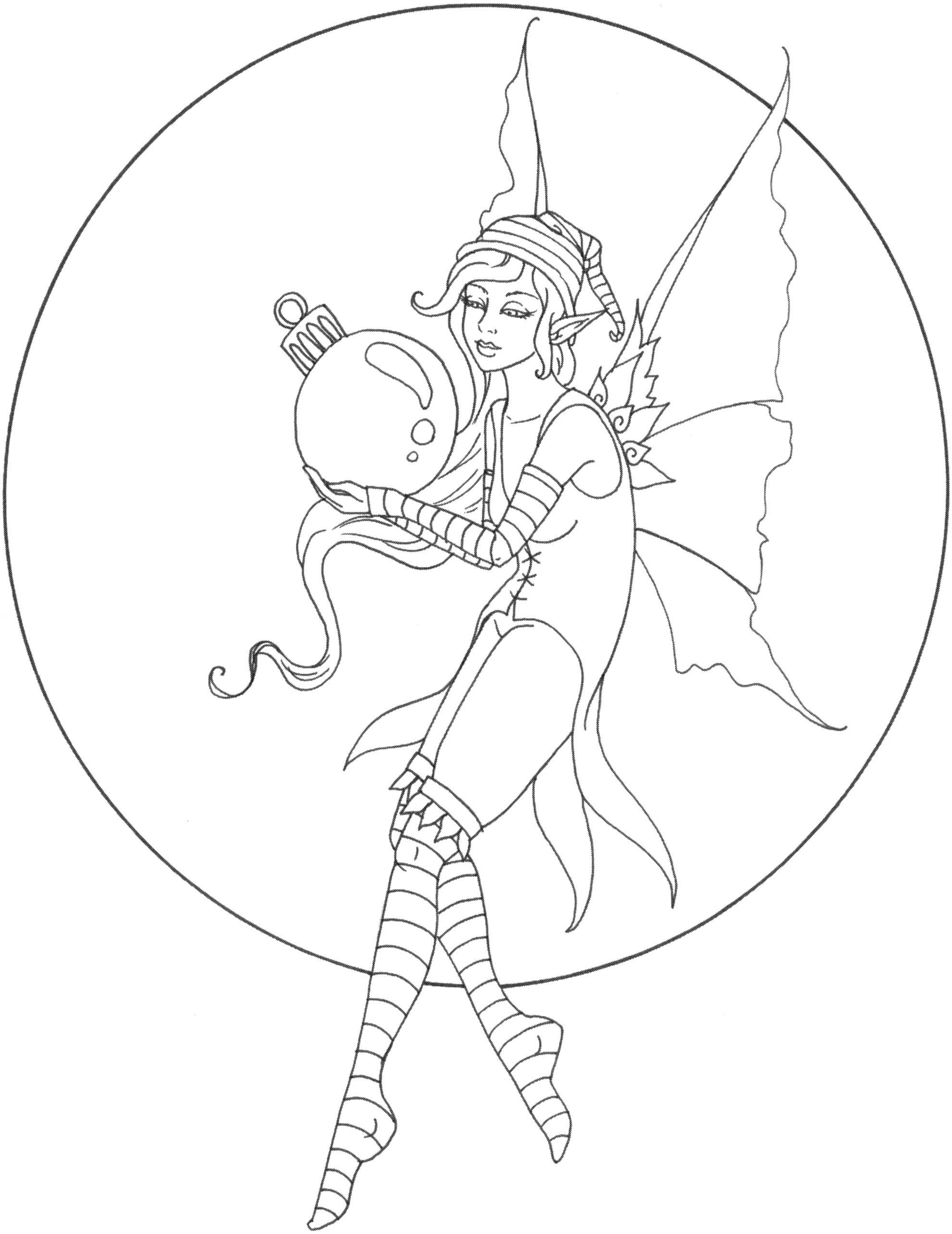

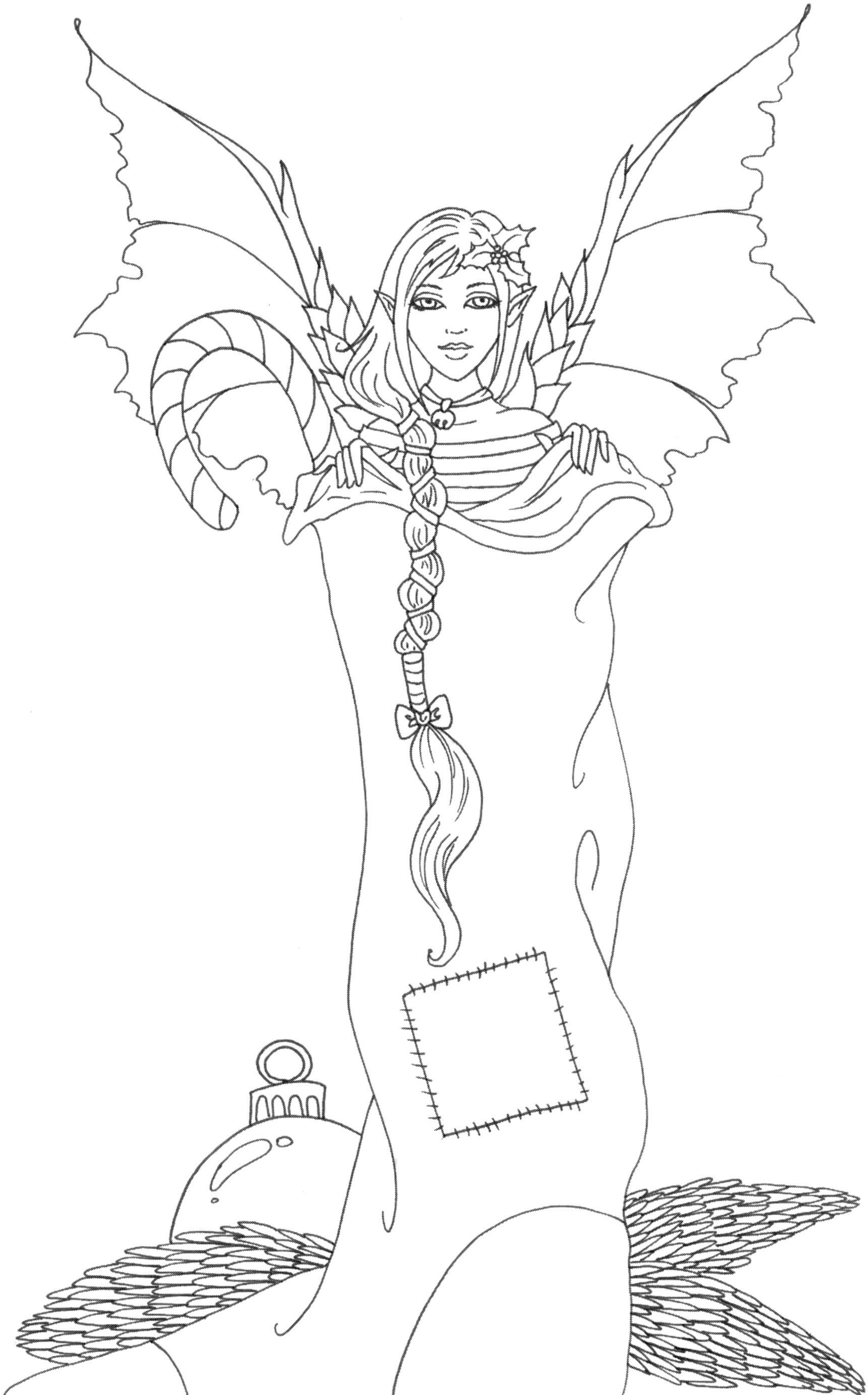

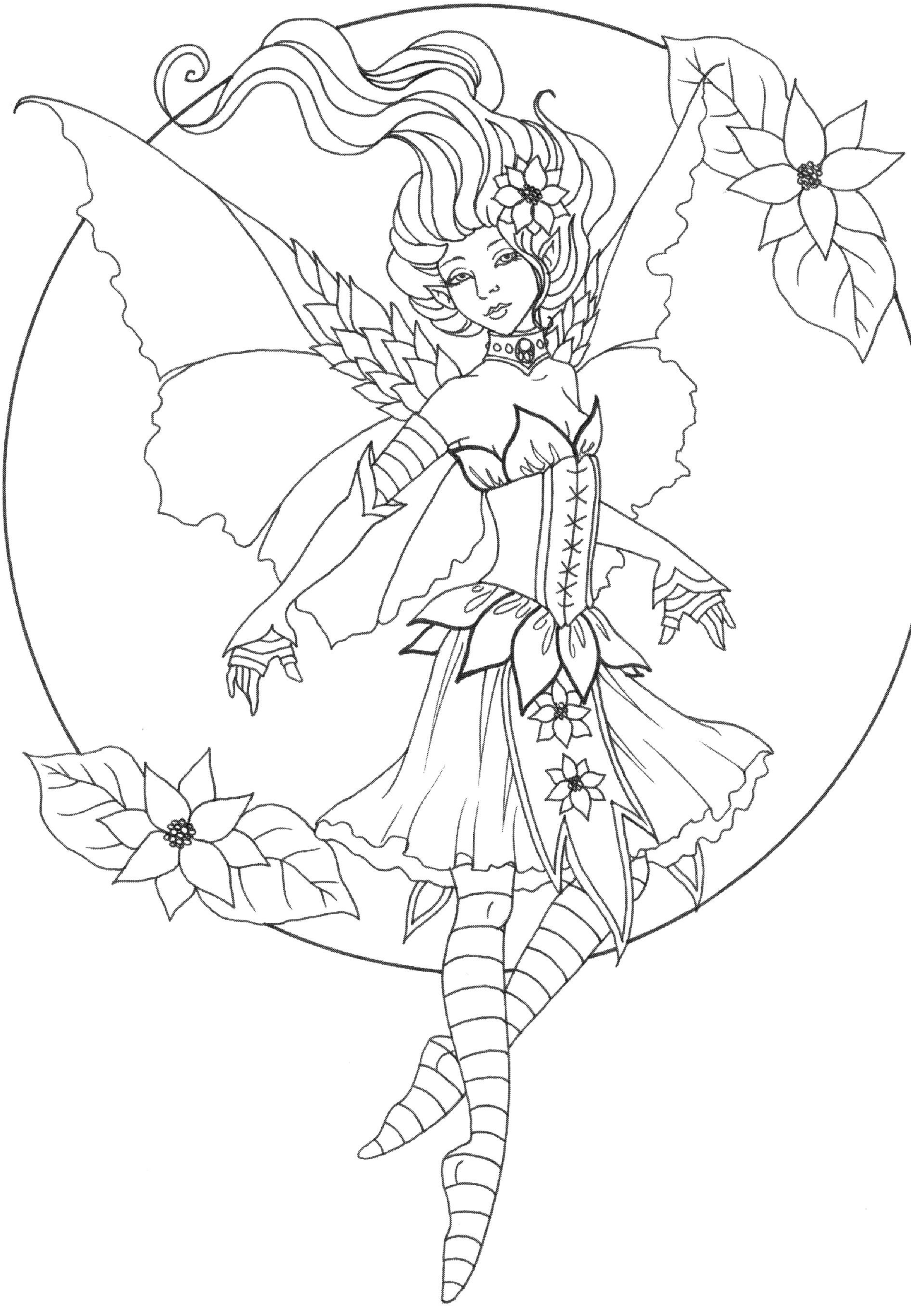

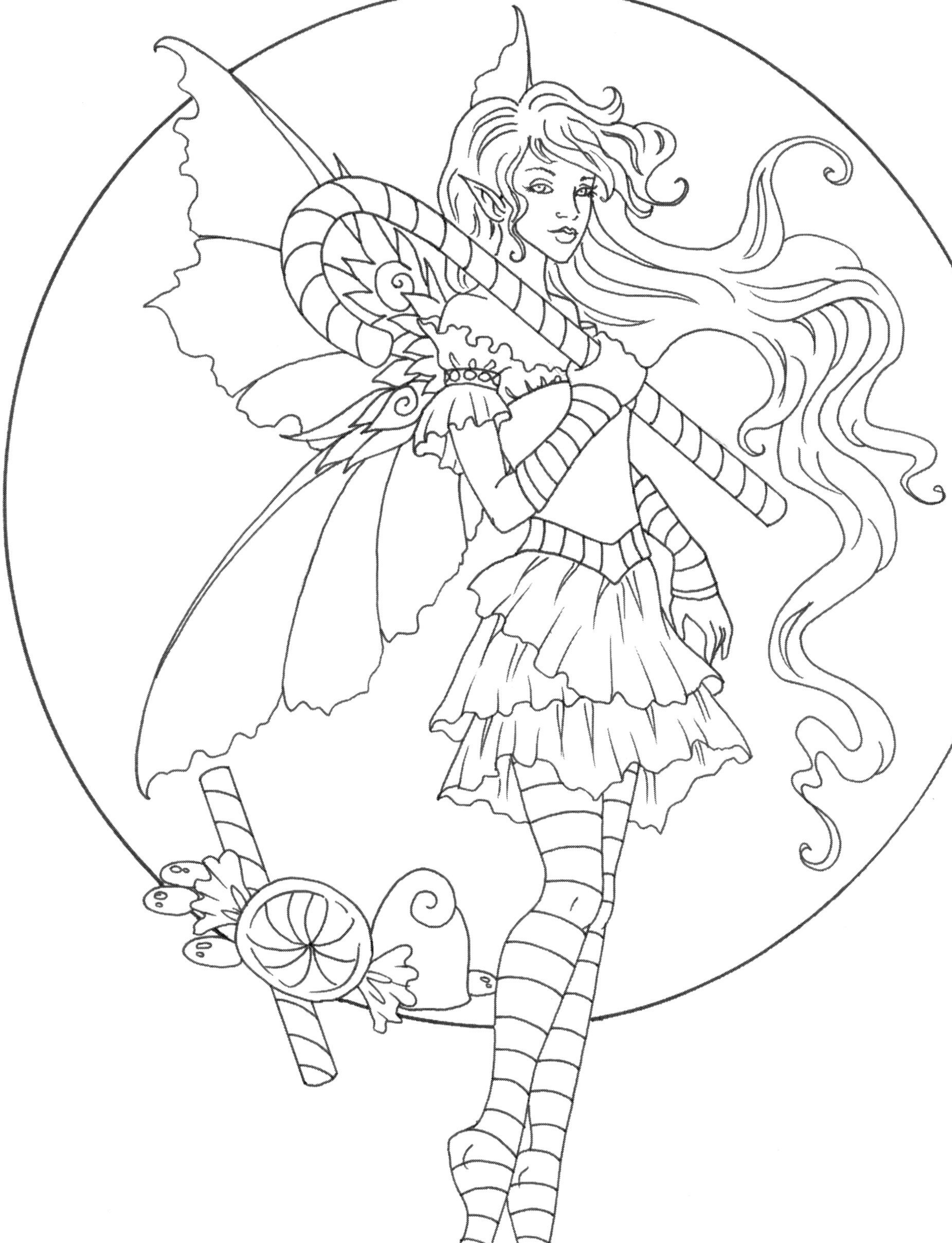

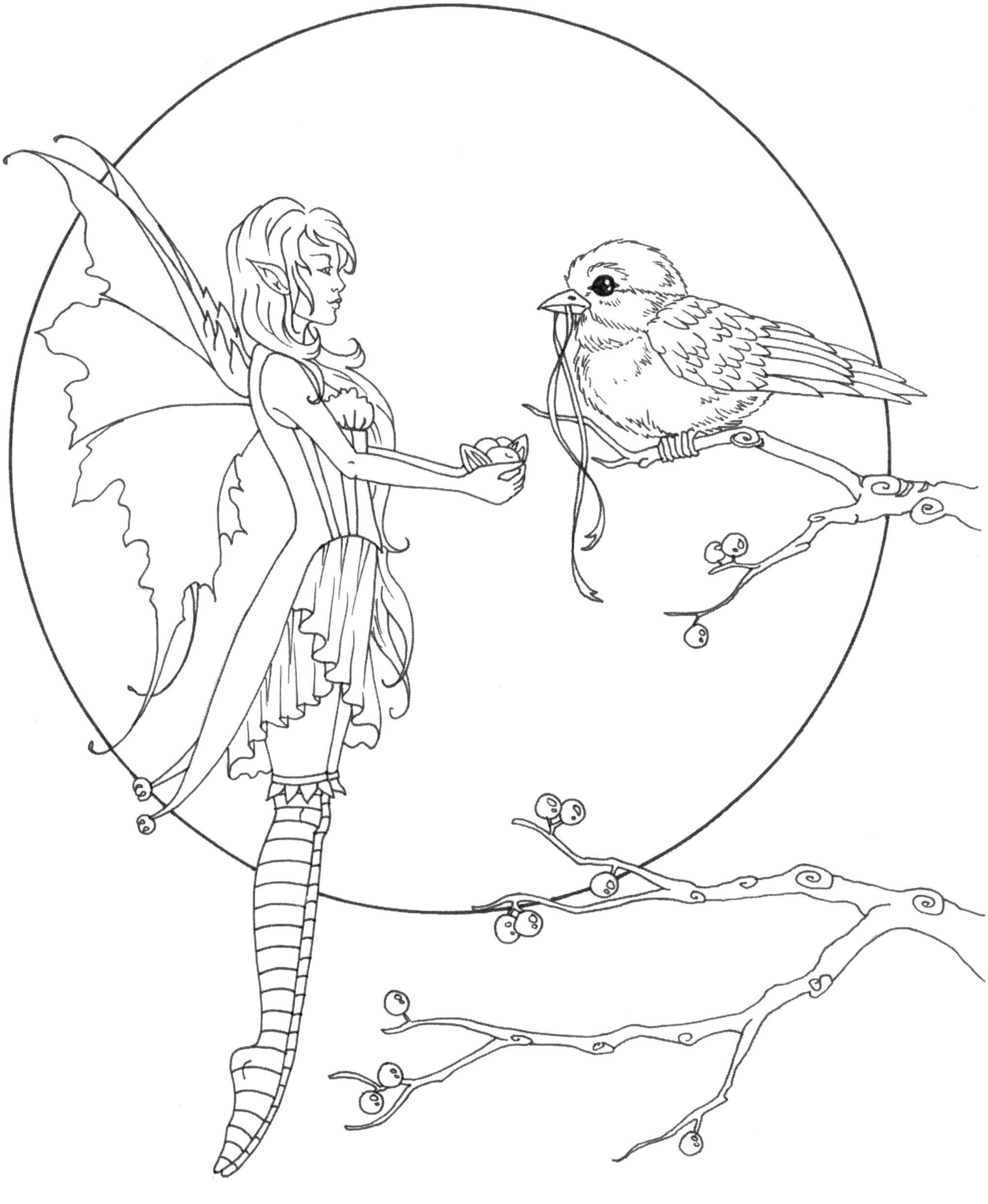

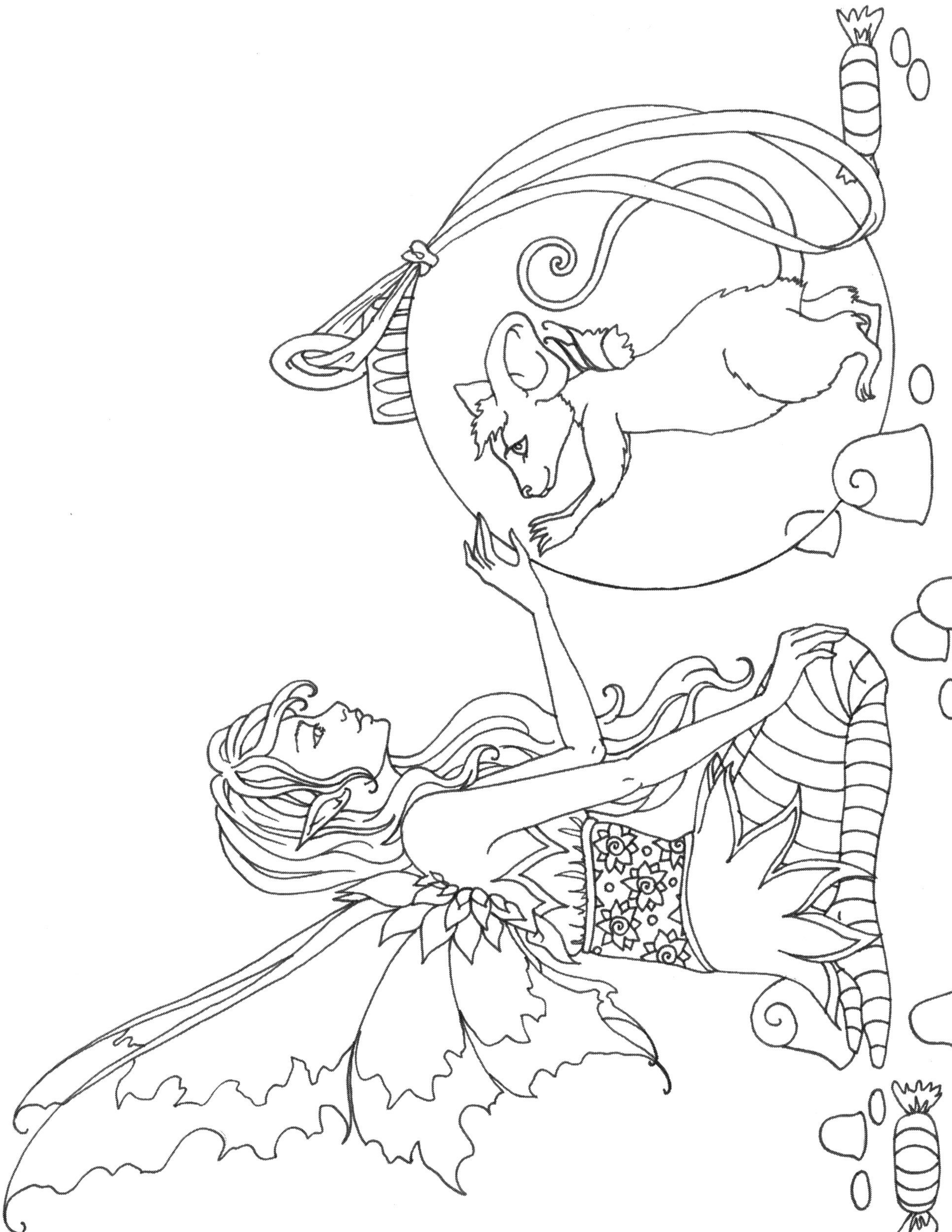

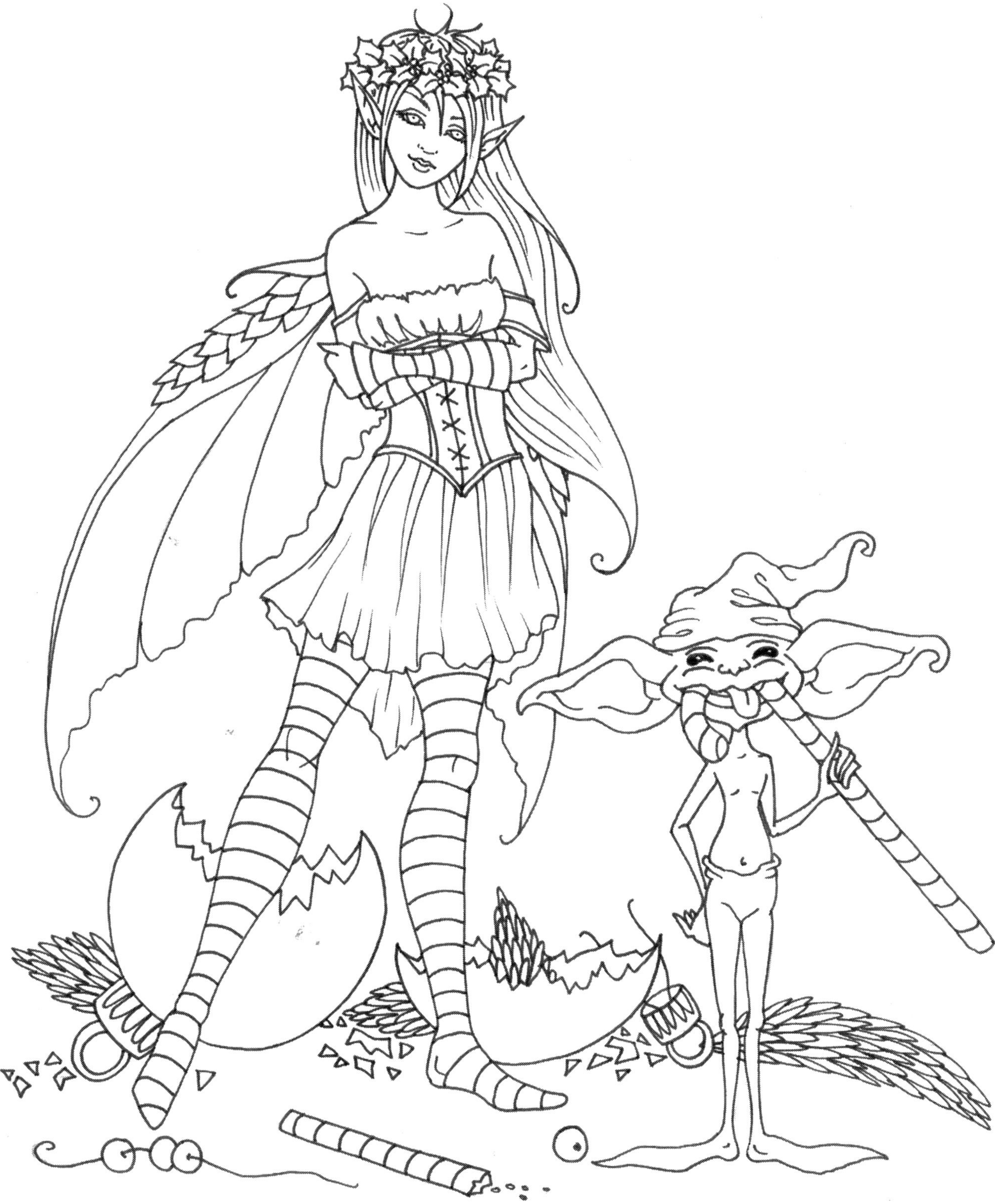

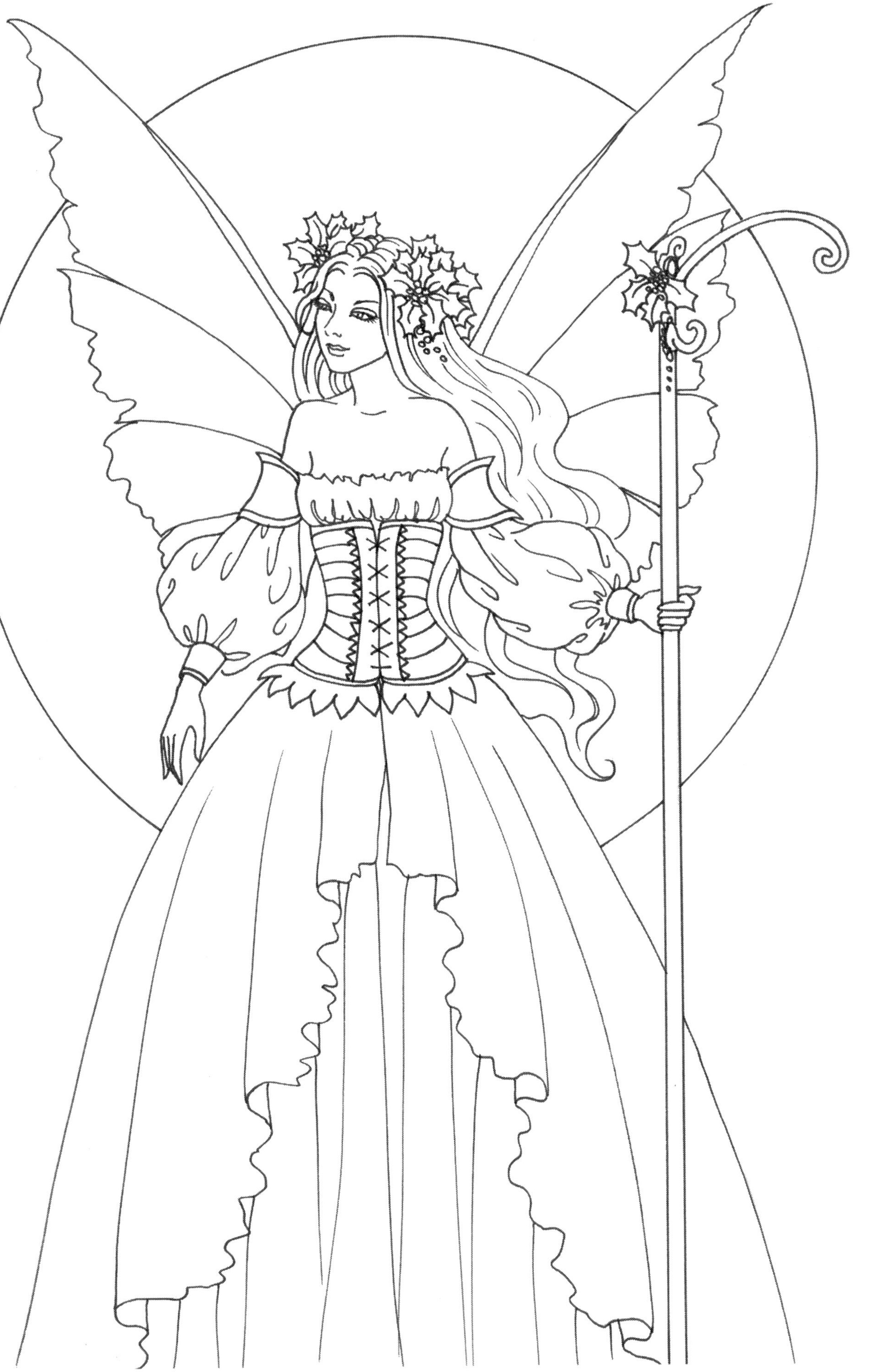

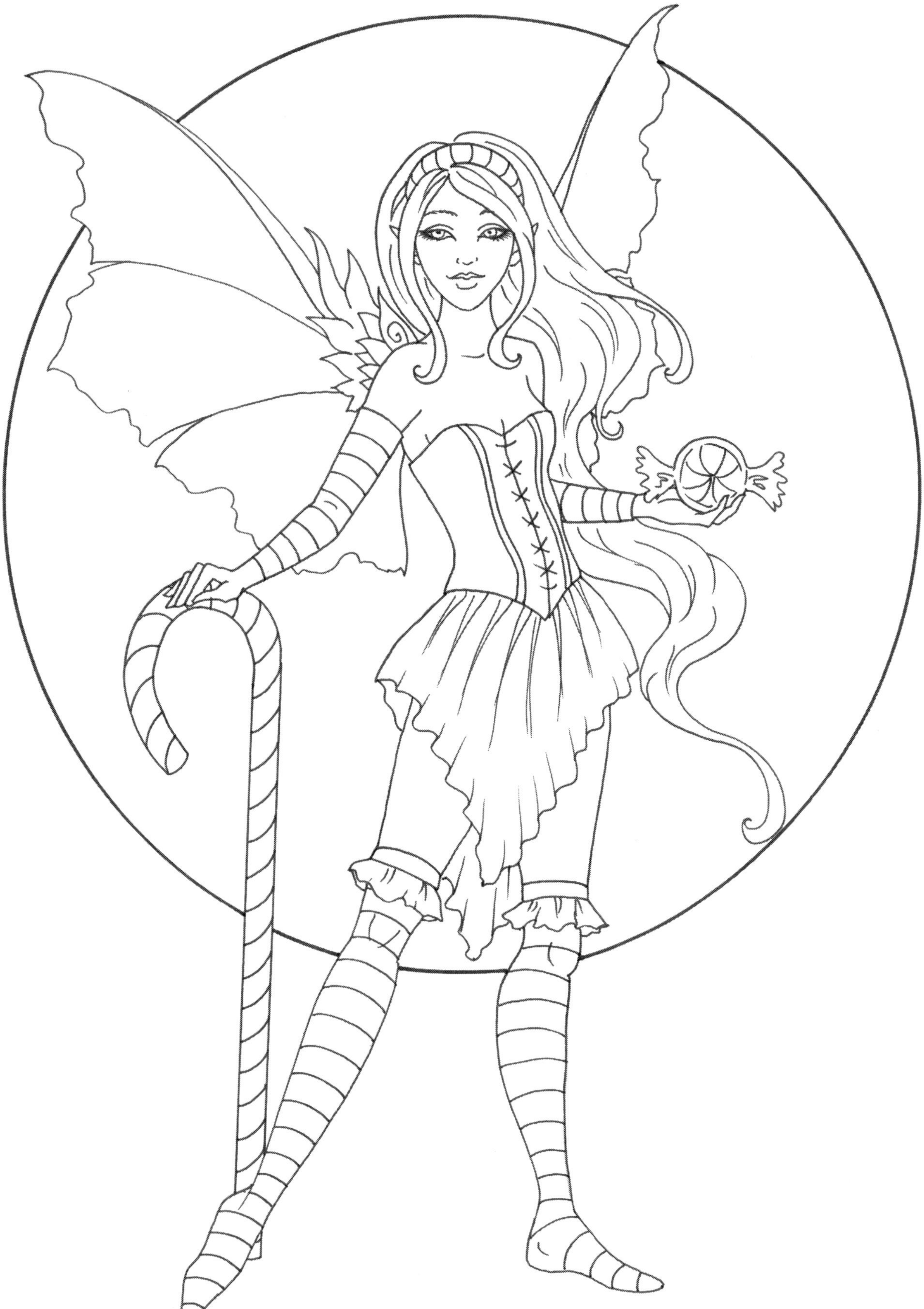

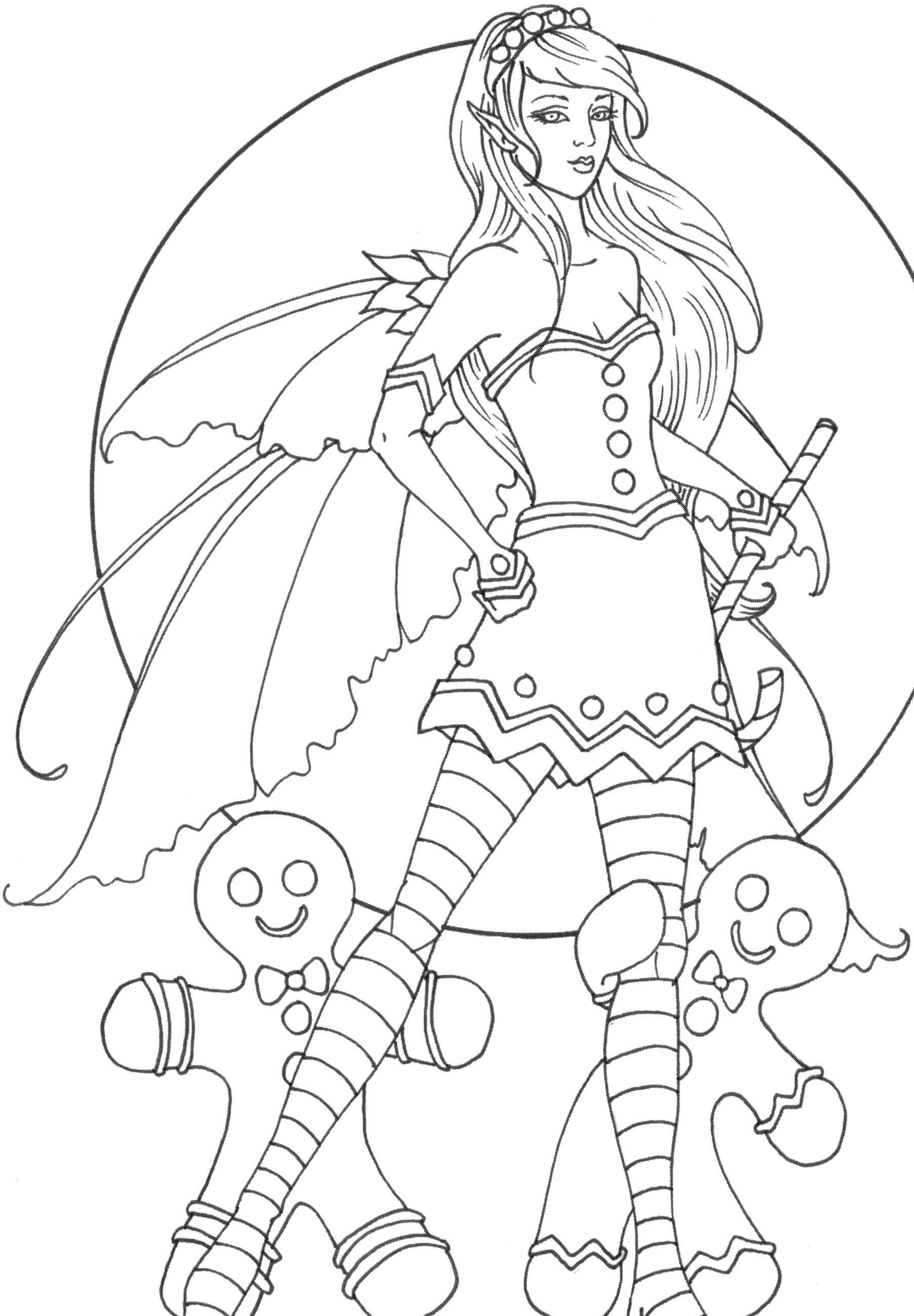

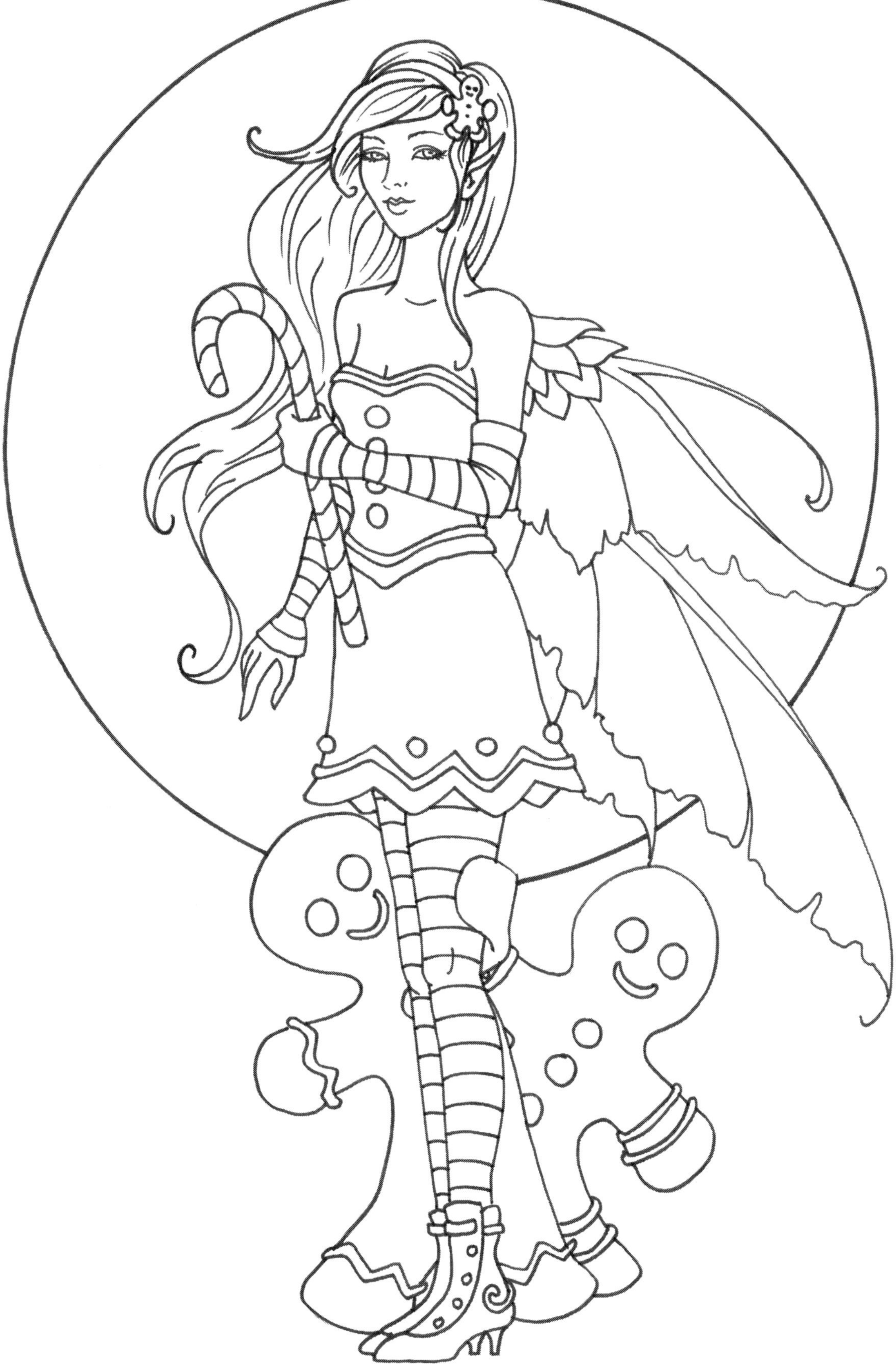

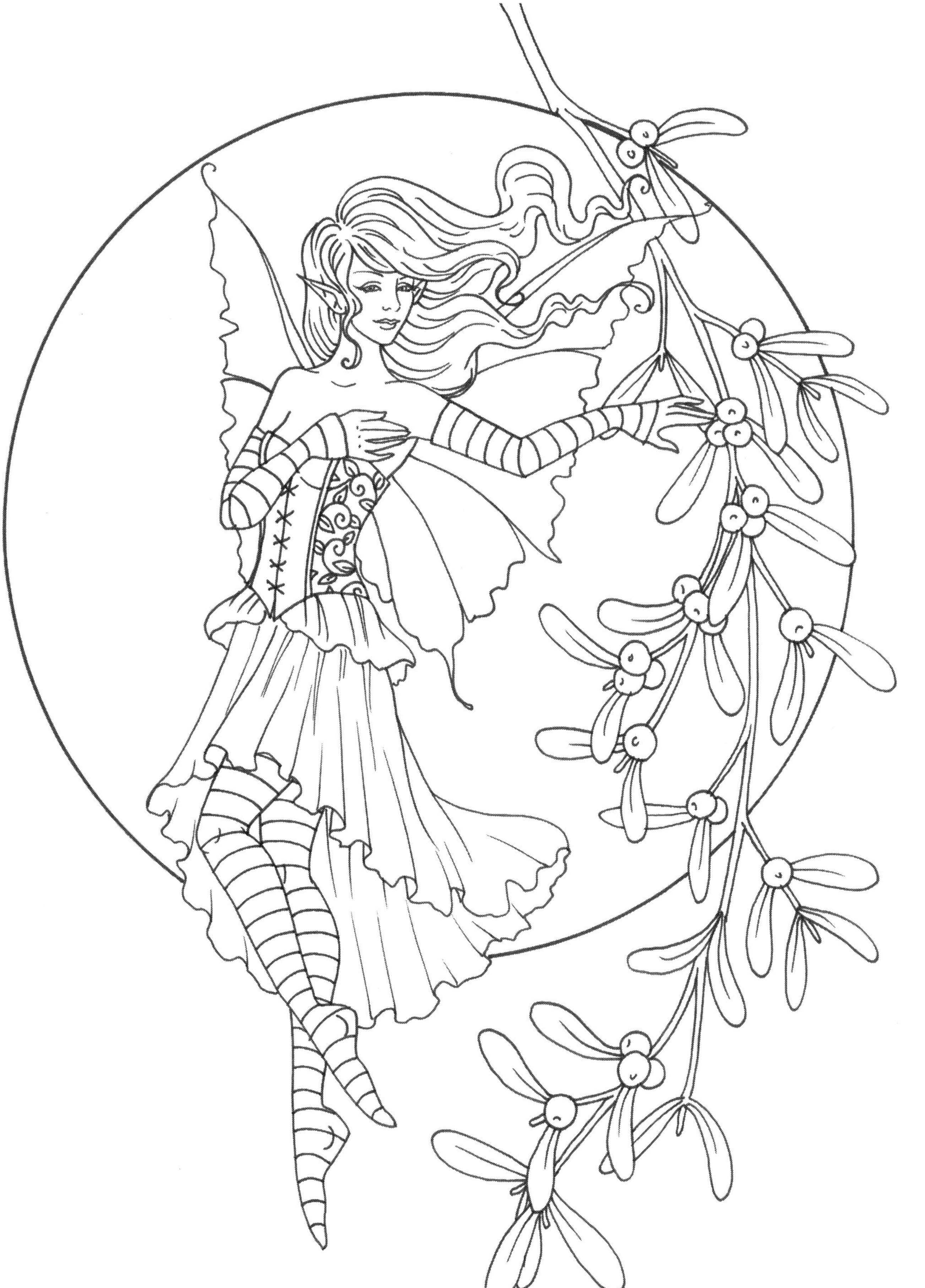

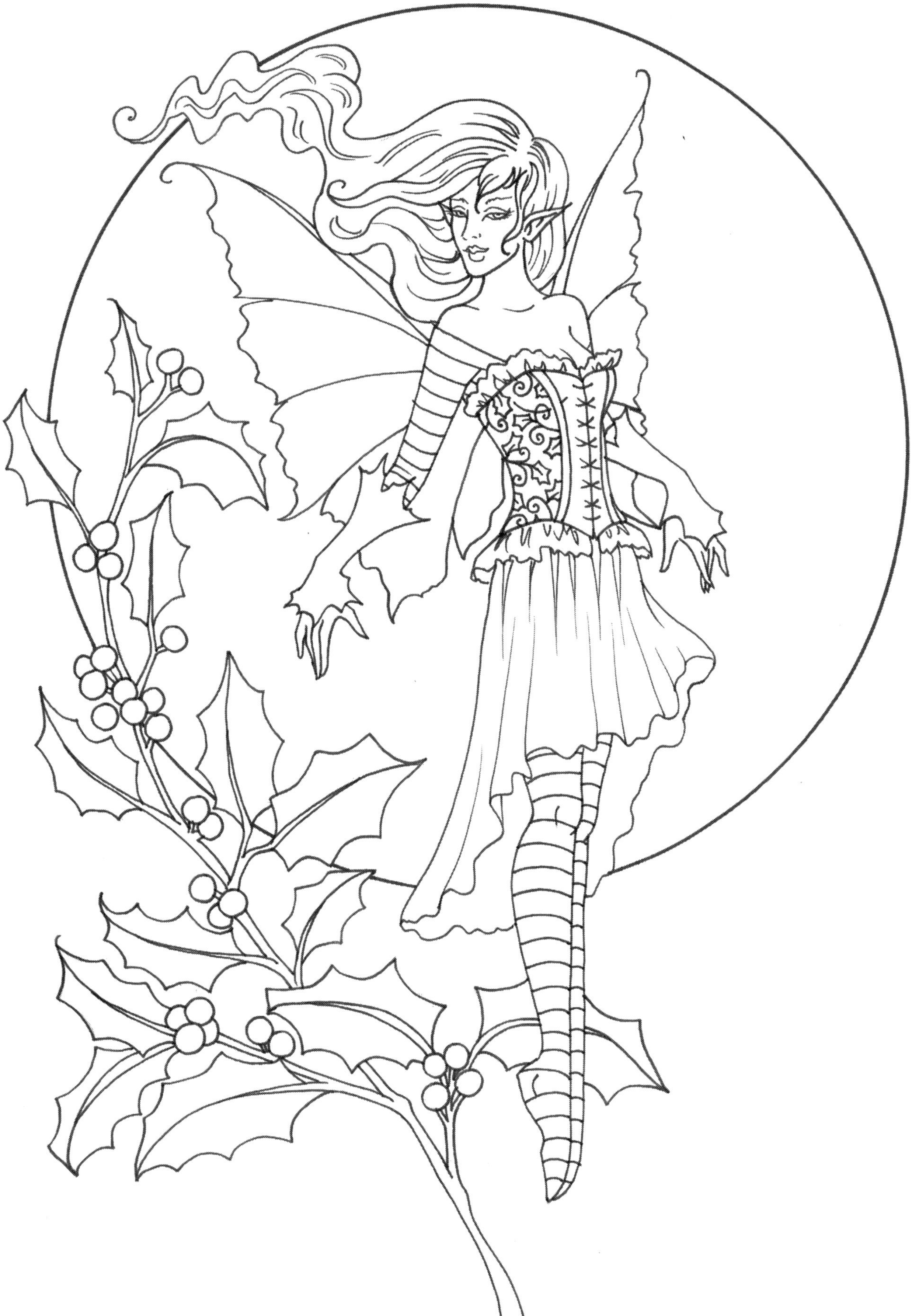

Made in the USA
Columbia, SC
10 July 2023

20228333R10024